Celebrations in My World

Earth Day

Molly Aloian

WE
RECYCLE

Crabtree Publishing Company

www.crabtreebooks.com

Crabtree Publishing Company

www.crabtreebooks.com

Author: Molly Aloian
Coordinating editor: Chester Fisher
Series and project editor: Penny Dowdy
Editor: Adrianna Morganelli
Proofreader: Crystal Sikkens
Project editor: Robert Walker
Production coordinator: Katherine Berti
Prepress technician: Katherine Berti
Project manager: Kumar Kunal (Q2AMEDIA)
Art direction: Dibakar Acharjee (Q2AMEDIA)
Cover design: Tarang Saggar (Q2AMEDIA)
Design: Ritu Chopra (Q2AMEDIA)
Photo research: Farheen Aadil (Q2AMEDIA)

Photographs:
Alamy: Jeff Greenberg: p. 25; Frances Roberts: p. 29; Dan Sullivan: p. 20; Visions of America, LLC: p. 8; David Young-Wolff: p. 21
Associated Press: p. 12
Classyflags: p. 16
Corbis: Bettmann: p. 5; Leland Bobbé: p. 27; Todd Gipstein: p. 17; JLP/ Jose L. Pelaez: p. 14
Earth Trustee: p. 10
Getty Images: Express Newspapers/Staff: p. 13; Time & Life Pictures: p. 15
iStockphoto.com: Amber Antozak: front cover (children around tree); Jani Bryson: front cover (children with globe)
Jupiterimages: p. 9
NASA: NASA STI (Scientific And Technical Information) Program: p. 4
Q2A Media Illustration: p. 28
Reuters: Jonathan Ernst: p. 22
Shutterstock: Ba Tu: p. 18; Rob Bouwman: p. 7; Claude Dagenais: p. 19; Mike Flippo: p. 26; Greenland: p. 30; Brian A. Jackson: p. 31; Morgan Lane Photography: p. 1; Dic Liew: folio glyph; Tyler Olson: p. 6; Denis Pepin: p. 24; Arne Trautmann: p. 23
Wowzone: p. 11

Library and Archives Canada Cataloguing in Publication

Aloian, Molly
  Earth Day / Molly Aloian.

(Celebrations in my world)
Includes index.
ISBN 978-0-7787-4288-3 (bound).--ISBN 978-0-7787-4306-4 (pbk.)

  1. Earth Day--Juvenile literature.
I. Title. II. Series: Celebrations in my world

GE195.5.A46 2009   j394.262   C2009-900230-2

Library of Congress Cataloging-in-Publication Data

Aloian, Molly.
  Earth Day / Molly Aloian.
      p. cm. -- (Celebrations in my world)
  Includes index.
  ISBN 978-0-7787-4306-4 (pbk. : alk. paper) -- ISBN 978-0-7787-4288-3
(reinforced library binding : alk. paper)
  1. Earth Day--Juvenile literature. I. Title. II. Series.

GE195.5.A46 2009
394.262--dc22
                                                     2009000324

Crabtree Publishing Company

www.crabtreebooks.com   1-800-387-7650

Published in Canada
Crabtree Publishing
616 Welland Ave.
St. Catharines, ON
L2M 5V6

Published in the United States
Crabtree Publishing
PMB16A
350 Fifth Ave., Suite 3308
New York, NY 10118

Published in the United Kingdom
Crabtree Publishing
White Cross Mills
High Town, Lancaster
LA1 4XS

Published in Australia
Crabtree Publishing
386 Mt. Alexander Rd.
Ascot Vale (Melbourne)
VIC 3032

Contents

What is Earth Day?

Earth Day is a holiday. People all over the world celebrate Earth Day on April 22 of each year. People have been celebrating Earth Day since 1970!

● Earth is the third planet from the Sun.

DID YOU KNOW?

*Earth is the only planet in our **solar system** that has people living on it. In the last 30 years, the number of people on Earth has increased by nearly three billion people.*

These people are at an Earth Day celebration.

On Earth Day, people celebrate our planet and bring attention to the need to care for the **environment**. In some cities, Earth Day celebrations last for an entire week! In 2010, people will celebrate the 40th anniversary of Earth Day.

Becoming Aware

People's actions harm the environment every day. As the **population** of Earth increases, people use more and more natural resources. They also dump more trash into landfills. This pollution is a serious problem.

People cut down trees and destroy natural areas.

DID YOU KNOW?

*Burning fuels such as coal, oil, and gasoline increases the amount of carbon dioxide in the air. High levels of carbon dioxide cause **global warming**.*

Every day, people pollute the land, air, and water. People clear land to make room for farms, roads, and homes. Animals that have homes on this land become **endangered**. The clearing of huge areas of land have put some plant and animal species in danger of becoming **extinct**.

The factory in this picture burns fossil fuels.

7

Helping Earth

People need to help Earth. Earth Day is the perfect day to do this! One of the best ways to help Earth is to reduce, reuse, and recycle.

- This mayor is speaking at an Earth Day event.

DID YOU KNOW?

Earth Day changes the way people think about the environment. People understand the need to protect the planet and all the living things on it.

Reduce means to use less. Reuse means using things more than once rather than throwing them away. Recycle is finding new ways to use old things. If everyone works together to help Earth, people will discover more ways to be "green." This means to be Earth friendly.

In Canada, people celebrate Earth Day, Earth Week, and Earth Month by recycling and caring for Earth.

9

Earth Day Origins

The idea for Earth Day began in 1969. An **activist** named John McConnell proposed the idea at a conference in San Francisco, California. An organization called the United Nations Educational, Scientific and Cultural Organization (UNESCO) discussed the idea of Earth Day. McConnell then created the Earth Day **proclamation**.

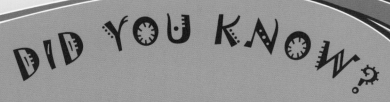

John McConnell proposed Earth Day to celebrate Earth's beauty.

DID YOU KNOW?

*Some cities celebrate Earth Day on March 20 or March 21. This is the first day of the spring **equinox**.*

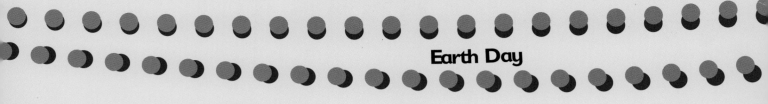

The proclamation said that people are responsible for keeping Earth clean. Several world leaders signed the proclamation. President George Bush signed it in 1990.

The document shown here is the Earth Day proclamation.

11

The First Earth Day

The first national Earth Day took place on April 22, 1970. Senator Gaylord Nelson planned Earth Day with the help of many others, including college student Dennis Hayes.

Gaylord Nelson was a senator from the state of Wisconsin.

DID YOU KNOW?

On Earth Day, people plan ways to make the air cleaner than it was in 1970.

Towns and cities across North America celebrated the first Earth Day. More than 20 million people joined in.

These people are celebrating the first Earth Day in New York.

13

Going International

Year by year, Earth Day grew. Schools planned events in honor of the day. Churches and businesses organized different activities. Teachers taught students how to reduce, reuse, and recycle.

Finding new ways to reduce, recycle, and reuse is a great Earth Day activity.

DID YOU KNOW?

The Earth Day Network (EDN) is an international group that grew out of the first Earth Day in 1970.

These college students are releasing a large balloon for Earth Day.

The first international Earth Day was in 1990. More than 140 countries took part in events. By then, over 200 million people celebrated Earth Day.

Earth Day Symbols

Earth Day has many **symbols**. One symbol is the Earth Day flag. The flag was designed in 1970 by John McConnell. It shows a photograph of Earth taken during the Apollo 10 space mission. The flag is made from recyclable fabric that is not damaged by weather.

• The ecology flag is shown here.

DID YOU KNOW?

On the ecology flag, the colors green and white represent clean air and green land.

Another Earth Day symbol is the green and white ecology flag. The shape on the flag is a combination of the letters "e" and "o." The letters stand for the words *environment* and *organism*. An organism is a living thing.

People wave flags proudly at Earth Day celebrations around the world.

Earth Day Decorations

Get creative when you are thinking of Earth Day decorations for your home or school. Use recycled materials, such as old cans or shredded paper, to make decorations that you can use year after year.

Paper grocery bags are Earth friendly.

DID YOU KNOW?

In 1994, more than 10,000 students from the United States and Canada decorated over 13,000 Earth Day paper grocery bags.

A few weeks before Earth Day, create
a huge mural for your classroom wall.
The mural will remind you and the other
students of the importance of Earth Day.

● This boy is
making a mural
for Earth Day.

Earth Day at School

Schools all over the world celebrate Earth Day in a variety of ways. Students plant trees and gardens. They organize land and river clean-ups. Some schools put on Earth Day plays or art shows. The more people you can get involved in Earth Day, the better!

These students are cleaning up a wetland area on Earth Day.

DID YOU KNOW?

Recycling newspapers, cardboard, and other paper products helps save trees.

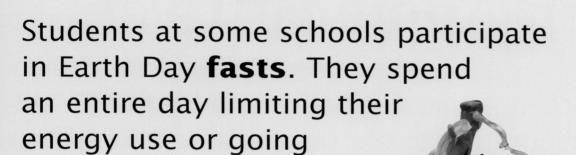

Students at some schools participate in Earth Day **fasts**. They spend an entire day limiting their energy use or going without energy.

These people are performing an Earth Day skit.

21

Green Apple Festival

The Green Apple Festival is the largest Earth Day celebration in the United States. The free festival lasts two days. Politicians, athletes, and activists teach people how to protect Earth. Schools and other groups show new ways to reduce, reuse, and recycle.

This band is performing at the Green Apple Festival.

DID YOU KNOW?

The Green Apple Festival tries to produce zero waste. They find ways to recycle and reuse their trash instead of throwing it away.

In 2008, there were eight festivals in parks across the United States. The festival is going into its fourth year.

Many people ride their bikes or walk to the Green Apple Festival events near them.

Other Events

Groups hold many other Earth Day festivals. These events help people learn more about keeping the environment healthy. Earth Day food festivals serve fruits and vegetables. They may also serve meats, cheeses, and other foods made in "green" ways.

- Fruits and vegetables are good for you, and growing them helps Earth.

DID YOU KNOW?

Today, more than one billion people participate in Earth Day events.

The Earth Day Network (EDN) is a group that plans thousands of activities to protect the environment each year. The network tries hard to promote a planet that is **sustainable**, or able to carry on.

These students are giving their school a green makeover.

New Laws

Since 1970, the government has passed new laws that help stop people from polluting air, water, and land. The United States Congress established the Environmental Protection Agency (EPA).

Today, endangered animals around the world, including these pandas, are protected.

DID YOU KNOW?

Gaylord Nelson is called the father of Earth Day. He was awarded the Presidential Medal of Freedom in 1995.

Cleaning up trash helps keep animals' homes clean and safe.

The EPA studies and watches environmental problems. It stops people from breaking environmental laws. It helps make new laws. For example, new laws protect animals that are in danger of becoming extinct.

27

Around the World

People of all backgrounds, faiths, and nationalities celebrate Earth Day. The day is celebrated around the globe! In 2008, in Caracas, Venezuela, youth groups from 15 different colleges presented their environmental projects at an Earth Day celebration.

This map shows places that have Earth Day events every year.

DID YOU KNOW?

On Earth Day in 1990, people in South America planted millions of trees.

In Nigeria, the Waste Management Society of Nigeria (WAMASON) launched a program to encourage people to stop littering. They began teaching people how to save their resources.

These children are planting a garden at their school.

All Year Long

People should celebrate and protect Earth all year long, not just on Earth Day. Many businesses now have recycling programs that help reduce waste. Organize a recycling program at your school if you do not already have one. Encourage your parents and friends to not use a car for a day or even a whole week. Start carpooling with friends and neighbors.

● Riding a bike is an Earth-friendly way to get around.

DID YOU KNOW?

There are many ways to help Earth all year long. Join a club in your area that cares about the environment.

Find other ways to reduce waste. Save energy and share what you have learned with your friends and family.

These windmills create wind energy, which is a sustainable form of energy.

Glossary

activist A person who takes action for social or political purposes

endangered Animals that are in danger of disappearing from Earth forever

environment Our surroundings including air, water, soil, climate, and living things

equinox The two times each year when day and night are of equal length

extinct Animals that have died out or have not been seen in the wild for 50 years

fast To go without something

global warming The increase of Earth's average temperature

population The total number of people living in an area

proclamation An official announcement

solar system The Sun and the planets, moons, asteroids, and comets that orbit around it

sustainable Able to be maintained

symbol Something that represents something else

Index

JUL 2 8 2010

32

Printed in the U.S.A. - CG